Words

sunil singh

ISBN 978-93-5610-653-6

Published in India 2022 by Pencil

A brand of
One Point Six Technologies Pvt. Ltd.
123, Building J2, Shram Seva Premises,
Wadala Truck Terminal, Wadala (E)
Mumbai 400037, Maharashtra, INDIA
E connect@thepencilapp.com
W www.thepencilapp.com

Author biography

sunil singh is poet based out of India . He finds his flight and sky to fly through writing . He has also performed at open mic poetry clubs in Mumbai, India. He writes on the mindset , the power of perception and context . He believes in the power of storytelling and how people consume stories as a species on the planet, deeply intrigues him .

CONTENTS

change

lot of things fades in life as we grow
like a faded sex in a long marriage
too good to be true things and people
are layered like onions with imperfect stories
metamorphizing perennially
it's just that ostensibly they look perfect
it is the grey spot on the black, white, or grey background
the context is everything
it can conjure up something
as excellent, diabolical or nothing

self esteem

the juncture when you throw the crutches
and decide to walk without them
you fall
you crawl
you get up
and just keep moving
until you start walking
and running
and all this happens
only because you decided to leave the crutches
that reminded you of your weakness
and insulted your self esteem

grace

i would call her grace
she was all bones and sharp edges
too tall
unpretty women who celebrated her flaws
with grace and confidence
and they appeared beautiful
the way she carried herself
like a skulking lone wolf in his den
wearing his scars like medals decorating his persona

sad little cockfights

the news channels
all they have is sad little cockfights
to keep people busy
or to confuse
or to digress their attention

think

when i think
i limit the infinite into my puny thought
when i give meaning
i bound the unbridled into a tethered sloth
i am a monkey of my own circus
i dance to the tunes playing in my mind
however i can choose to learn better tunes
tunes that will lead to the dance i dream to perform
it will still be a finite version of the unknowable infinite though

twenties

in my twenties early and later
all i did was
got stoned drunk and had loads of sex on beaches
dirty or pristine didn't matter
sitting naked
pink like a boiled shrimp
with a grotesque shade of red
in the sunlight
that flew sweet and yellow
like a half-finished cheap champagne sitting too warm to be swigged
i made a good use of youth
i wasted it like a horrible deflating sorrow
and was high like helium filled sense of living
and spoke about love music and poetry
and wasted every day as much as possible

martini and manhattan

we went to alfredo's
i ordered a martini and
she a manhattan
our conversations bowered each other
till the cheery and olive were still alive in the respective poisons
then we plucked them out and shared
she left with a piece of olive and i with a piece of cherry

get drunk on life my friend

sit back with a bag of popcorn
to binge the rom com that life brings on
sometimes sit with martini
pick the olive and bite it
while musing on the nostalgic flashbacks
enjoy the drink with a slice of life
say life is hard or easy or whatever for the sake of narrating
your transient point of view
gulp down everything
that life brings
to the last sip
get drunk my friend
it's fun
that's the way to live

carapace

everyone said
i am without a skin
and i should be shameless and thick skinned
the intimidations and embarrassing situations
created a carapace around my aura
now i laugh off the offences
and my smirk is my defense

words

words are magical
i build my future with the bricks of words
i visit my past on the vehicle of words
i create my own meaning out of words
i live my life inside the mansion of words
i pull the wool over my eyes
i spin the yarn telling myself
all is well
is it not or is it
well i manipulate the power not pejoratively
of understanding what i want to hear

ukraine

the whole world should revolt
we all should come on the roads
and scream our lungs out
to restore peace in ukraine
today it's them
tomorrow it could be you or me
if humans won't speak for the humanity
who will

perception

a permutation and combination of 86 billion cells in my brain
lands me in dilemma whether to go toward or away from something
the bedrock or the meat potatoes motives behind my every perception is survival

beyond obvious

listen
always look for something that's beyond obvious
there's a story that's hidden inside a story
some tears hidden behind a poker face
a bleeding dream in the garb of a smile
a child crying inside about to scream through the tears
and an adult consoling it with a straight face
swallowing the pain
so that the emotions don't show
afraid of the vulnerabilities
wrapping the emotions like a child in a cocoon of all is fine
safe from the predators
see
the stories that aren't available for sale in the market
like a portrait an artist makes for art
the stories that are silently peeking out of the eyes
mismatching the yarn that we spin to the world
behold things by changing the context

social chameleons

people all around
different sizes and shapes
cladded differently in fabrics of wool and words
everyone trying to put their best foot forward
with a façade of smile and confidence
trying to match the environment
social chameleons with placid mien
selling themselves to buy a space among others
to feel belonged respected and trusted
driven by the ulterior motive of fame and monies

broken confidence

how do you build a broken self-confidence
when life has been harsh on you
and punched you back-to-back
when the people who were with you
become against you
when the storm of life
destroyed the love respect and trust
when you feel small and beaten down
how do you build self-confidence
when all the fingers are pointed towards you
when you feel used and unwanted
how do you live
when your surviving has become an insult
how do you smile and be confident
when people are staring at you
like a stigma
a bad influence
when all you wanted to be was a good man
with love respect and trust
how do you fight a life that has chosen to beat you down
to shit
how do you enjoy the journey of life
when the companions are treating you like a disease

fly

i am scared for they know me know
if i try to fly they will mock and bring me down
however i will fly
i had given me in the hands of someone
whose wish could have bloomed or withered my existence
and those hands are left with nothing but tales
of our togetherness from dusk to dawn
and dawn to dusk
leaving the melancholy yarns behind
i will carry the happier ones for they are light
when i take shelter after a flight
will ruminate in the tales of our togetherness
and share them with the world
so that people believe love is not a responsibility
it is soft like a whisper
light like a feather
beautiful like a blooming flower

perfect

why you pick excuses to sulk
to stare at me as if i have committed a cardinal crime
this is who i am
i come with my flaws
like everyone else
like you
like something real
which is more attractive than the imagined reality
for you are busy looking for a magician
and you miss the magic that's happening every moment
real is broken flawed crook
small round tall black white yellow
real is what you perceive it is
as real as the permutation and combination
that the cells in your brain can make it to be
real is subjective at the mercy of your observation
do you ask a river to flow in a certain way
why would you ask me to exist in a certain way
can you just let me live the way i am
i am already in struggle with myself to live the way i am
you can live the way you want
we can live together living our individual life
you me and our differences
we three can stay together

the expiry date of trust love and respect

love is eternal
trust is the bedrock
respect is earned and can't be bought
is but a load of baloney floating around
the fact is
people change
they stop loving you
trusting you
respecting you
they have fine lines with expiry dates
beyond which they call it quits
there's only one truth
money
that's it
if you have money
it's easier for people
to like you
to love you
to trust you
to respect you
it's all fake and superficial
our whole existence is selfish and monstrous
parasitical in nature
that's what it is
our puny existence has only one purpose

survival
our every decision is based on that hard layered intent

monsters

sometimes the people you trust the most
gives the deepest wounds
who you trust with your feathers
cut them so that they don't lose you
sometimes the people who you want to take for the world tour
cage your flights and break your confidence as a person
they make you quadriplegic
so that you will forever depend on them
and never leave them
when you like a flower
you pluck it
when you love it
you let it exist on the plant
sometimes people only like you
because you are useful to them
they want to use you till you fulfil their selfish ulterior motive
and you think it's love which you don't understand
and which you don't want to take for granted
and you go deeper in the quicksand
a trap you can't escape ever
sometimes a friend is the most dangerous human being
that you will ever encounter in life

crocheting

how moms take measurements
and starts knitting a sweater
at the end of every day she knows what comes next
end of one day knits into the next
and finally she winds up with a garment
flexible and strong
similarly we can build a bridge to the next day
knowing what comes next
is like crocheting

flexible tradition

let's tweak the tradition to match individuals
and not individuals to match the tradition

day & night

day wanes night waxes
cold evenings
moon appear
stars twinkle
night wanes
day waxes
sun appear
cold mornings become warmer
day shines

situation

sometimes i want to hit a home run out of yankee stadium
however it's my hubris
swing-for-the-fences
a dangerous mentality
just with a single act
i want the change to be colossal
metamorphizing my life for good
the situation is like
the bare-bones resources
to be caught on the run
which couldn't be counted on
to be at my beck and call
a feeling like getting hanged
takes my mind into flow state

existence

not complaining about anything at all
and not criticizing anyone at all
being grateful for everything
and giving importance to everyone
being kind
being nice
tired of fighting with everyone and everything
including myself for the life i wanted for
now just want to accept the life i have
and live
just live

late night radio station

late night radio station
egg poaches in olive oil and bread
the rusty room
frogs crocking outside the window
crickets chirping
late night rickshaw rides for ice creams
rationing one cigar for a week
sharing cigarettes
food
and the moist winds in the winters
the smell
the temperature
the memories

idea

generate an idea
retain it in a poem
infer the soul it has
transform it into a higher purpose
like write a book
or script or hundred other things
do something about it
don't let it rot like a big fish in a small pond

bird

a painter sees colours of a bird
a musician listens to music of a bird
an actor studies the carriage of a bird
a dances sees how it moves waddles and flies

story

it's only a story at the end
my fear
and my only wish
i wish i live a good one
does it really matter

greed

why there's so much of greed in this world
people trying to use people
shameless megalomaniacs
parasites gorging each other
cannibals
everybody knows this ain't gonna last
still trying to rob and steal and fill their coffers

respect

one life
self-respect is not for discount

life

so much for a dream
we know it's not real
still so much for it
we fool ourselves to keep us busy
add some theatre to it
we want lemonade when it's raining vodka
and vodka when it's raining lemonade
guess we like controlling
playing almighty
or maybe we keep trying to grab back control
rebelling perpetually
with an ulterior motive of control

insomnia

is it a guilt
of not having done best
longing for the dawn to start hustling again
is it a fear
that i will lose control of the realty
if i fall asleep
these insomniac nights
is like an endless maze
that never gets solved
and the day breaks

tears of joy

sometimes in life
on a gloomy day
i see something beautiful
something light like love
and i smile
and tears of joy appear in my eyes
sometimes in life
when i am feeling low
i hear a beautiful song
that touches my soul
and i smile
and tears of joy appear in my eyes

you

you were the soil to me
basic
earthy
elemental
you were home
a place where i was always welcomed
a thought that you will always be there
gave me freedom to venture out
be bold
daring to fall flat on my face
you were a cocoon
i lived inside you

love your fate

we want to be blessed with a wonderful fate
everything comes as a complete package
we want we like and not what we don't
accept everything holistically
embrace the thorns with love
and enjoy the beauty of roses
be grateful for the fate that we have
wonderful or not who cares
it's the only one we have

good bad and ugly

life is good bad and ugly
where you focus it grows
whatever we want in life
it is already there
we need to focus on it to see it and grab it

stories

we are just stories
under the umbrella of more stories of culture religion society family
these umbrellas are like crutches
that support our journey
whether we act or sing
dance or paint
run a business or a nation
we are organizing things and people
to give meaning to our work
to create a beautiful story
that people can relate to
confused in the chaos of where we come from
and where we go
stories are the bedrock
a lullaby that soothes our journey
with meaning and purpose
while we are here

path

right path or wrong
there's no path
we all walk differently
and create a path where there was none
only in the hindsight
we perceive the path as right or wrong
however our perception is subjective
it's only a path
neither right nor wrong

one sided love

i loved her
she loved me
what a beautiful world it was
just two of us and the rest of the world
and then she left
and took that world with her
the ruins are there
and i still live there with her
but she doesn't live there anymore

silence

words uttered
often gets misinterpreted
whereas silence is like an empty canvass
it's a respect you give to the listener
to paint it with a choice of his/her colours
that's the irony of a language
at times it complicates what's simple
whereas silence is like an unfathomable ocean
agile tranquil colossal and powerful

see

we see things close up
at an arm's length
and from a wider perspective
there's a story in abstract
a fiction in a non-fiction
something in nothingness

is greed good or is it bad

it changes people
like a chameleon
people tend to support some one
who could satiate their greed
is greed good or is it bad
i do not know the answer to this too
it's one of those umpteen unanswered questions
but greed surely hurts
when you are betrayed for greed

weave

till you get a space
till it's your time
weave the home of your dreams
choose the fabric
the colours the views
make your home in mind
and when it's time
and when you get a space
paint the canvass
let the magic takeover

writing

this is just to write
to put some words
to persevere when you have nothing to say
to respect the writing process
to penetrate the writer's block
this is just a respect to the process of writing

friend

a friend is not just a person
however a feeling
friendship is not a relationship
however a beautiful story

paper boats

its pouring heavy
rain puddles popping out everywhere
let's make a boat out of papers
and row in the puddle waters
it's been a while for our boats to be anchored on
the clouds of imagination
a home on earth
sounds better than a castle in heaven

dawn

got darkness galore in this part of the town
let's focus in the light that the dawn will bring

help

is there anyone who doesn't need help
we all are travelling in the same cavalcade
our outside might appear different
however there's a parity to how we look and fell inside
pain and pleasure equally affect us
helping each other is a communication
saying –
i feel you
don't worry
i am there
and we will go through this together

abundance

7.8 billion people
no inadequacy of air to breathe
is there scarcity on the planet
or a mindset of scarceness

fear

the slow poison
that paralysis the soul and body
no-fear is the secret attitude
no matter what life brings
never be afraid of anything

butterfly

whatever is chased flies away
whatever is loved will come back home

surviving

beaten tired and washed away
with the torrents that life has been throwing
tired of hoping that the light will shine
at the end of the tunnel that seems everlasting
the books from the shelves collecting dust stare at me
will i be able to read them like before
worked up with the chaos
propelled by the bedrock necessities of life
the artist in me longs for the art
all i do is breathe and survive
while my heart longs to live a life

an artist

i am an artist
i am the disease of the society
i am like a pearl which is the disease of the oyster
we both are born out of
perpetual abrasive irritation of our milieus
when a religion chef against religion
class against class
ignorance against intelligence
puritanism against pleasure
white against black
jingoism against internationalism
fascism against communalism
price against value
sale against service
suspicion against trust
death against life
and out of these rigid dichotomies
emerges my voice
on a tight rope of morality and nihilism
i am an artist
i am a pearl miscast before swine
i paint sing narrate act
and the message i bear is simple and basic
whatever releases people and brings them together is good
and whatever confines and separates them is bad

i show how the culture is a eunuch
pornography is his severed balls
thermonuclear weapons his staff of office
sadder than the eunuch is its balls
deadlier than the impotence is murder
i am an artist
i am the disease of the society
i am like a pearl
which is the disease of the oyster
we both are born out of constant abrasive irritation of our milieus

love without chasing

the most beautiful things
are simple
everything is simple
and beautiful
success like a butterfly
will come and sit on us
if it's loved without being chased
whatever is chased flies away
whatever is loved will come back home

rooster

the morning rooster crowing loud
cock-a-doodle-do
behold everyone i have just got a new day for you
this place called world is surrounded by roosters of different shape and sizes
responsible for the success in markets and at home
because of so much crowing around it's commercialized
and the only rooster that crows with more energy melody and conviction will be preferred
for the sun will shine
a rooster crows or not
however to conjure up the appearances of something that's absent we need someone to take responsibility for the sunshine
so we can blame him/her for no sunshine
and conveniently roast too every now and then
and certainly when it's christmas time

ocean

you can tell me all your secrets
and let them disappear in my fathomless depths and
i won't say a word to anyone
you can say anything under the sun to me
and all i will do is listen without uttering a word
nothing is permeant here
even the footprints in the sand
gets washed by the waves at the coast

better halves

no free lunches on earth
in love i was your lunch
and you were mine
two wholes came together
now you and me are one half each
losing our other halves
to become each other's better halves

self-respect

i respect you and
i respect myself
if respecting me is cumbersome for you
i will move away to make it light for you
to a place where i can feel at home

joke

you were used as a pawn
in a political plan
and now people are mocking you
for the joke you have become
they spoke
innocently picking pearls out of what they uttered
i answered
i am happy i was used
to add laughter and smile to someone's life

travelling with love

where do you plan to go with so much love in your heart
they asked
with the simplicity of a two year old i answered
where others are heading with hatred in theirs
love feels lighter
i love travelling light

www.ingramcontent.com/pod-product-compliance
Lightning Source LLC
LaVergne TN
LVHW050421160726
843469LV00041B/1177

* 9 7 8 9 3 5 6 1 0 6 5 3 6 *